Learning to Plan
and Be Organized

Published by

M A G I N A T I O N   P R E S S ®

An Educational Publishing Foundation Book
American Psychological Association
750 First Street NE
Washington, DC 20002

Magination Press is a registered trademark of the American Psychological Association.

For more information about our books, including a complete catalog, please write to us, call 1-800-374-2721, or visit our website at www.apa.org/pubs/magination.

Book design by Susan K. White
Printed by Lake Book Manufacturing, Inc., Melrose Park, IL

Library of Congress Cataloging-in-Publication Data

Names: Nadeau, Kathleen G., author. | Beyl, Charles, illustrator.
Title: Learning to plan and be organized : executive function skills for kids with AD/HD / by Kathleen G. Nadeau, PhD ; illustrated by Charles Beyl.
Description: Washington, DC : Magination Press, [2016]
Identifiers: LCCN 2016012500 | ISBN 9781433822179 (hardcover)
ISBN 1433822172 (hardcover) | ISBN 9781433822131 (pbk.) | ISBN 143382213X (pbk.)
Subjects: LCSH: Attention-deficit hyperactivity disorder—Juvenile literature. | Attention-deficit-disordered children—Life skills guides—Juvenile literature. | Planning—Juvenile literature. | Orderliness—Juvenile literature. | Executive ability in Children—Juvenile literature.
Classification: LCC RJ506.H9 N327 2016 | DDC 618.92/8589—dc23 LC record available at https://lccn.loc.gov/2016012500

Manufactured in the United States of America
10 9 8 7 6 5 4 3 2 1

Learning to Plan and Be Organized

EXECUTIVE FUNCTION SKILLS FOR KIDS WITH AD/HD

by Kathleen G. Nadeau, PhD
illustrated by Charles Beyl

MAGINATION PRESS • WASHINGTON, DC
American Psychological Association

Contents

To Parents and Other Adult Helpers

Planning and being organized are two important "executive functioning" (EF) skills, those all-important skills that we need to set goals and accomplish them. The ability to regulate emotions and the ability to control impulses are both executive functions. The ability to direct and sustain attention is also an executive function. While not all children that struggle with executive functions have AD/HD, all children with AD/HD struggle with executive functions.

Executive functions are, in large part, controlled by the pre-frontal lobes of the brain, a part of the brain that doesn't fully develop until our late 20s. That is why we associate good executive functions with maturity. Our brains are better able to make plans, monitor our progress, control emotions and impulses that tend to distract us from our long-term goals, and modify plans appropriately when circumstances change or new information becomes available.

EF skills are much stronger when a child reaches young adulthood if he or she has been working to develop them all along the way. For example, children learn the basics of impulse control in preschool. "Keep your hands to yourself," "use your inside voice," "use words, not fists," and "stop and look both ways" are but a few of the phrases we teach children to help them develop impulse control.

Practicing good habits, developing routines, learning to organize materials, managing time, and building working memory are all key executive functions that are covered in this book.

Learning to Plan and Be Organized is geared for children in elementary school. The text and exercises in this book are AD/HD-friendly. It is illustrated with cartoons to hold your child's interest, highly readable (even for kids who don't like to read), and divided into chapters, so that the book can be read in smaller portions. It is intended for parents to read with their children. It can also be used as a guide for school counselors and other professionals.

This book includes forms and checklists for building a new habit; creating morning, after-school, and bed-time routines; and planning a project. These forms are also available as free downloadable PDFs on the book's page on Magination Press's website: www.apa.org/pubs/magination.

Because this book has been written for elementary school students from first through fifth grades, you'll need to use your judgment as a parent about when your child is ready to master certain skills or habits. In general, encourage your younger child to master the "early skills" first. These are skills such as:

- getting to bed on time
- practicing the morning and bedtime routines until they are smooth and easy to follow
- keeping his or her room neat
- remembering to "tie the bow"—picking things up and putting them back after he or she uses them
- paying attention to what time it is
- paying attention to what day it is and checking the family calendar so that your child knows when special things are coming up

Once your child is in fourth or fifth grade it's time to add more planning and organizing skills. So once they've mastered the "early skills," then it's time to focus on:

- keeping track of time so that your child is on time without reminders
- setting reminders for him- or herself to stay on track
- becoming independent when doing their homework and chores
- starting to use an agenda to keep track of homework and upcoming events

Focus on learning one skill at a time. If your child enjoys this book, there's no problem in reading it from start to finish. But, as you begin working on helping your child to develop these EF skills, focus on just one at a time. Be patient and encouraging. Reward your child's improvement. Don't wait for perfection.

The keys to success are to:
- make these exercises enjoyable,
- set reachable, age-appropriate goals,
- encourage your child if he or she struggles,
- reward your child with recognition and praise,
- and reward your child with privileges and tangible rewards if your child needs more motivation.

EF skills are important for success later in life. Remember, these skills are developed over the course of years. I hope that this book will be an engaging and enjoyable way to help your child build confidence and competence in managing the tasks of his or her life.

Just for Kids!

Life is full of lots of things that we need to keep track of, and that's not easy. We learn to do it little by little. Remember when you were three years old? Nobody expected you to know what time it was, or to remember to brush your teeth. Your parents didn't expect you to get dressed by yourself or to come down to breakfast without a reminder.

Now that you are older, you have more things to keep track of—like bringing in money and a permission slip for a school trip, or remembering to bring your soccer uniform and cleats to school so that you can go straight to soccer practice afterwards.

This book will help you get better at planning and organizing—organizing your things and organizing your time. When you are good at planning and organizing, your day will run smoother, with fewer upsets and problems.

Many of the kids that find it hard to plan and be organized have something we call attention-deficit/hyperactivity disorder, or AD/HD. Sometimes it's just called ADD. All kids have to learn to be more organized and remember to get things done, but it's harder when you have AD/HD because the part of your brain that helps you plan and be organized is kind of "sleepy." The "sleepy" part of your brain makes it difficult to keep your mind on what you are supposed to be doing. With your "sleepy" AD/HD brain you might start doing something else and forget what you were supposed to be doing in the first place. AD/HD can also make it harder to stick with things until you finish them. And finishing things is a very important part of being organized.

Kids with AD/HD can be very smart and creative. They may think up cool ideas that other kids might never think of. Sometimes, when you have a great imagination and have AD/HD, it's hard to keep your mind on what you're doing because your brain is always thinking of lots of interesting things.

There are many things that you can do to make your days run more smoothly. And there are lots of ways that your parents can help you get better at remembering, planning, and getting things done. We'd like you to read this book with your parent or some other adult so that you can talk to them about what you read.

Your parents bought you this book because they want to help you get better at planning and organizing. Planning and organizing isn't just about doing things you don't enjoy so much, like cleaning up your room or doing homework. Planning and organizing is important so that you can get things done that you want to do. For example, if you want to make

brownies, but you forgot to plan and make a list of all the things you need to make them, you won't be able to make those delicious brownies and eat them! But if you make a list of what you'll need, maybe with a little help from your mom or dad, then you'll make your delicious brownies and be happily eating one!

Planning and organizing includes things like:
- planning projects,
- organizing your things,
- remembering what you need to do,
- figuring out how much time things take,
- keeping track of time so you get places on time,
- finishing things that you start,
- sticking to things that are hard at first,
- and solving problems instead of just getting frustrated.

These are all things called "executive functioning skills." That's a big term that means knowing how to accomplish things. This book will help you get good at these skills. And, you know what, if you learn these skills, you'll be able to reach your goals!

No two kids are alike. In the next section of this book, you'll find a checklist called "A Checklist About Me." Read each item with your mom or dad, and check off the items that describe you. Once you understand the things that are a bigger challenge for you, you can figure out where to start in building new skills with your mom or dad.

CHAPTER ONE

A Checklist About Me

The following checklist is a collection of things that other kids with AD/HD have said about themselves. Going through this checklist can help you think more clearly about yourself. It will help you understand the things you are very good at and the things that you are having problems with. Going over your answers with your mom or dad is a good way to figure out which skills you need to work on.

Now, take a minute to check off the things that apply to you. You might already do some things really well, but need help in other areas.

There are no right or wrong answers—this is all about you!

My Habits

❏ It's hard for me to develop a new habit and stick to it.

❏ I'll practice a new habit for a few days, and then I start to forget about it.

❏ I feel bad when my parents or teachers criticize me when I forget a habit.

❏ Even when I try hard, I still keep forgetting habits like turning in my homework when I get to school.

My Morning Routine

- ❑ When it's time to get up I usually feel tired and want to sleep longer.

- ❑ I run around in the morning looking for something I need to get ready for school.

- ❑ Sometimes I miss the bus or am late to school.

- ❑ I get off track in the morning instead of getting dressed and coming downstairs for breakfast.

- ❑ Sometimes I forget something I need for school and have to call my mom or dad to bring it to me.

- ❑ Sometimes I don't eat breakfast because I don't have time.

My After-School Routine

- ❑ When my mom or dad asks me to do a chore after school I usually forget.

- ❑ I just lie down and watch TV after school instead of doing homework or chores.

- ❑ I usually feel tired after school and don't want to start on my homework.

- ❑ I put off doing my homework unless my mom or dad makes me do it.

- ❑ It seems to take me forever to finish my homework.

My Bedtime Routine

❑ I usually stay up later than I ought to and don't get enough sleep.

❑ I have trouble falling asleep at night.

❑ I forget to brush my teeth unless I am reminded.

❑ I don't usually lay out my clothes for the next day before I go to bed.

❑ Sometimes I play games on my phone or iPad after I'm supposed to be asleep.

Organizing My Stuff

❑ My bedroom is usually a big mess.

❑ My parents get mad at me because I don't clean up my room.

❑ I don't really know where to put everything when I try to clean it up.

❑ I have a lot of stuff in my room that I don't really use any more.

❑ When my parents tell me to clean up my room I don't know where to start.

❑ My clothes drawers are all a big jumble, so it's hard to find what I'm looking for.

Getting Things Done

❑ I really want to get things done, but then I fall off track.

❑ I forget about things that I need to get done.

❑ I plan to do something, but then I tell myself I'll do it later.

❑ It's really hard for me to start on a big project.

❑ It's hard to make myself do things that are hard or boring.

Managing My Time

❑ I am often late getting ready to go out somewhere.

❑ I lose track of time, especially when I'm watching TV or playing video games.

❑ I'm usually rushing at the last minute instead of getting ready ahead of time.

❑ Homework always takes me longer than I think it will.

❑ I usually wait until my mom or dad tells me it's time to do something.

Planning Projects

❑ It's hard for me to get started on a big school project because I don't know where to start.

❑ I usually start on projects too late and have trouble finishing them on time.

❑ Usually I have to ask my mom or dad to get something for my project at the last minute because I didn't think of it before.

❑ I always think that I can finish projects more quickly than I really can.

❑ My parents tell me I need to learn to plan ahead next time I have a big project to do.

Remembering Things

❑ I forget things that my mom or dad tell me.

❑ I don't write things down—I just try to remember them in my head.

❑ It's hard for me to remember to tell my parents about something they need to do for school, like money or permission slips for a field trip.

❑ I forget to ask my parents to get something I need for a project.

❑ I forget where I put things.

What I Wish People Understood About Me

☐ When I forget to do something, it's not because I don't care.

☐ I really do need a lot more reminders to help me remember.

☐ I always have thoughts in my head that distract me from my routines.

☐ I wish my parents would help me find solutions instead of getting mad at me.

☐ When my creative brain turns on, my organizing brain seems to turn off.

☐ It may look like I'm not trying, but I really am.

☐ I get discouraged when people only point out what I'm doing wrong.

☐ Hugs and encouragement help me get back on track.

CONGRATULATIONS! You've finished the checklist. It's a good idea to talk to your mom or dad about your answers. Did they agree with your answers? Were they surprised by any of your answers? It may feel like you've checked off an awful lot of things to work on, but...

Don't worry!

Help is on the way!

This book will tell you about lots of ways to make your day go more smoothly so that you're not always rushing or upset because you forgot something. There are lots of ways that your parents can help you and lots of ways to learn to help yourself.

Now, if you're like a lot of other kids, you're getting a little tired of talking about ways to get organized. That's okay. It's good to take a break after you've been trying hard and concentrating hard. "Concentrate" means trying really hard to pay attention.

Time for a Break!

Wow! You have learned a lot about getting organized already. You've earned a break. See if you can spot the words hidden in the word search below!

H C F Q C M R B G T
X A R W M C L E A N
R A B I T O N D T M
T Q T I M E D T P G
D Z F N T R E I A T
T W L F U R J M T Q
B F S U D S E E N H
K R L G N P T A Y K
L I E P K C L Z B T
D N T A L P H X R F
S K G B K F W X T R

TIME
PLAN
HABIT
CLEAN

LUNCH
BEDTIME
BREAK

Do you feel better after your break? Taking a break is a good habit to learn. You'll get a big task done more easily if you take little breaks every 20 minutes or so. For example, if you're doing homework or cleaning up your room you'll get more done if you work hard for 15–20 minutes and then take a five-minute break. Your mom or dad can set a timer so that you know when your break starts and when it onds.

Things to do during your break:

- Sing a song.
- Do 15 jumping jacks.
- Talk to your mom or dad.
- Take 10 deep, slow breaths.

Things *not* to do during your break:

- Watch TV.
- Start playing a video game.
- Go in another room and start playing with your brother or sister.

These aren't good activities for a short break because you'll get involved in your game or TV show and then won't want to stop and go back to doing homework or cleaning up your room. These kinds of activities should be used as rewards after you've finished your homework or clean-up project.

You've done enough for right now. **Good work!**

CHAPTER TWO

Building Good Habits

THROUGHOUT this book, we are going to teach you to create lots of different daily habits, because life just goes easier when you have developed good habits. When something is really a habit it becomes automatic and you don't even have to think about it, you just do it.

How to Form a New Habit

So the first thing this book will teach you about is how to form a new habit. It takes about a month to form a new habit if you practice it every day. Here are 11 steps to building a new habit.

Tie your new habit to an old one.
If there is something you already do automatically, it will be easier to learn a new habit if you tie the new habit to the habit that is already established. For example, if you want to remember to take your vitamins every morning, and you already have the habit of brushing your teeth after breakfast, then you can "tie" the vitamin habit to your tooth-brushing habit by placing the vitamin container next to your tooth brush. That way you'll see it and remember to take your vitamins before your brush your teeth.

Make the habit as easy as possible.
Make sure that you don't have to take
unnecessary steps to perform your new habit.
For example, if you need water to swallow your
vitamins, be sure that you keep a plastic cup in the
bathroom next to the vitamin container. That way
you don't have to go in the kitchen to find a cup
to take your vitamin. Another way to make your
vitamin habit easier is to use chewy vitamins that
you can just pop in your mouth and chew without
needing water.

 Make the habit hard to ignore.
While you're building your habit, make it
hard to forget to do it. For example, you might
keep the vitamin container on the bathroom counter
next to your toothbrush and away from any other
objects on the counter so it doesn't get "hidden"
in clutter.

 Put reminders everywhere.
Create as many reminders as you need to. For
example, as a reminder to take your vitamin,
you could put a sticky note on the bathroom mirror.
You could even put a sticky note on your toothbrush!

Practice the new habit 10 times in a row.
This doesn't mean take 10 vitamins on the same morning. It means you would go into the bathroom, pretend to take your vitamin, pretend to brush your teeth, and then leave the bathroom and do it all over again—10 times. It might feel silly while you're doing it, but you are building muscle memory that will make it seem "normal" to take your vitamin before you brush your teeth!

 Imagine doing the new behavior.
Did you know that imaging something over and over is almost as good as doing it over and over? So, for example, before actually doing your morning routine, it's helpful to sit and imagine yourself doing each step of the routine.

 Practice "instant corrections."
An "instant correction" is going back and doing your new habit the minute you remember that you forgot to do it. If you're not at home when you remember, then write yourself a reminder note to do it the minute you get home from school.

 Get back on the horse and ride.
Just as you should get back on a horse if you fall off, you should get back to building your habit if you fall off track. If you've forgotten to take your vitamin for a few days, just start taking it again. Get back on that horse and ride!

9 **Problem solve if it's not working.**
If you do all the steps we've talked about and you're still forgetting to take your vitamin, don't give up! Problem solve! Maybe it's not the best plan for you to take your vitamin in the bathroom before brushing your teeth. Talk to your mom or dad and see if you can come up with a better plan. Maybe you should keep your vitamins on the table where you eat breakfast, for example.

10 **Practice the habit 30 days in a row.**
Keep a chart of each time you take your vitamins and track your new habit until you have succeeded 30 days in a row.

11 **Reward yourself!**
You'll need encouragement along the way. Tell your mom or dad when you've succeeded for one whole week so that they can congratulate and encourage you. Plan a small celebration when you've completed two weeks, then three weeks. And plan a fun reward when you've completed all 30 days.

Pick a New Habit

So, now that you've learned how to build a new habit, it's time to pick a habit to work on.

Talk to your parents and make a list of new habits that you'd like to work on so that your days run more smoothly. Then pick one to try first.

Write your new habit on the habit chart on the next page.

Use stickers and stars so that it's fun to keep track.

And don't forget to talk to your mom or dad about your rewards!

Congratulations! You're on your way to building good habits that will make your days feel better.

My New Habit

Name of new habit: _____

Old habit I'll tie it to: _____

How I'll remind myself: _____

	Did it on time	Remembered and did it later	Did it after a reminder
Monday			
Tuesday			
Wednesday			
Thursday			
Friday			
Saturday			
Sunday			

Way to go! And remember, if it's not working, then it's time to problem solve. Tie it to a different habit? Make more reminders? Do it at a different time of day? Keep problem solving and you'll get there!

Time for a Break!

Can you think of a habit that you already do really well? Draw a picture or write about it here:

CHAPTER THREE

Your Morning Routine

IN the last chapter, you read about developing habits. Now, this chapter is going to teach you about developing routines. A habit is a single action you do automatically—for example, brushing your teeth. A routine is several habits that go together in a chain—that is, a group of habits you do in the same order every day.

Routines are good because once you practice a routine, you don't have to think about it very much. Routines help you organize your time each day so that you get all of the important things done.

In this book, we're going to help you build three important daily routines:

 Your morning routine

 Your after-school routine

 Your bedtime routine

Let's begin by talking about your mornings. When your morning goes well, you're off to a good start and things are more likely to go well later in your day.

Having a good morning really starts the night before. Why? Because the most important part of having a good morning is getting a good night's sleep so that you're not tired. You'll read more about how to develop a good bedtime routine in Chapter 5.

How do your mornings usually go?

Lots of kids feel tired in the morning and don't get up on time. And then, once they are up, they have trouble getting ready because they can't find what they need. After getting up late and then having trouble getting ready, some kids rush out the door before they have a chance to eat a healthy breakfast.

Is this what your mornings are usually like?

Follow the steps in this chapter, and pretty soon you'll have calm, happy mornings.

Create a Morning Checklist

The first step for building a morning routine is to think about all of the things you need to do in the morning. Talk to your parents and come up with a list of what you need to get done before you get out the door each morning.

It may help to work backwards from the time that you need to be out the door. Be realistic! If your bus comes at 8, you probably want to leave your house at 7:45, not 7:59.

Once you have figured out what you need to do each morning, work with your mom and dad to create a checklist.

Your list might look something like this:

1 Get up at 7.

2 Get dressed.

3 Make my bed.

4 Comb my hair.

5 Come downstairs for breakfast around 7:20.

6 Eat breakfast.

7 Brush my teeth.

8 Put my homework and my lunch in my backpack.

9 Put on my shoes and jacket (if it's cold out).

10 Head out the door at 7:45 to have plenty of time to walk to the corner and catch my bus that comes at 8.

My Morning Checklist

Use the morning checklist in the book as a guide as you write your morning activities. Talk to your mom or dad about what order you need to do the items in your morning routine in. Then write them on this chart and put your chart where you'll be sure to see it each morning. Some kids have one copy in their bedroom or bathroom as a reminder and another copy in the kitchen to check off each morning.

Morning Activity	Mon	Tue	Wed	Thu	Fri
1					
2					
3					
4					
5					
6					
7					
8					
9					
10					

Check off each activity you've completed each morning before you leave for school. If there is something you keep forgetting to do, it's time to create reminders or change your routine. The more you practice, the easier it will become to follow your routine. Good luck!

Put your morning checklist on the fridge, or somewhere else where you will see it each morning. Each morning, you and your parents can check off the activities that you do on time. By the end of the first week, you'll probably start getting the hang of your new morning routine!

Get out of Bed...on Time!

The first step in any kid's checklist is getting out of bed. Lots of kids have trouble getting out of bed in the morning. How about you?

If you are always tired in the morning, that's a sign that you need more sleep. We'll talk more about this in Chapter 5 about creating a bedtime routine.

In addition to making sure you're getting enough sleep each night, here are some ideas to help you get up more easily in the morning:

- Set your alarm clock to go off 15 minutes before you need to get up. This will give you some wake-up time to stay in bed without making yourself late to school.
- Ask your mom or dad to get you an "artificial dawn" light. This is a light that starts off very dim and gradually gets brighter so you wake up more naturally as if the sun were waking you up. This can be very helpful in the fall and winter when it's still dark outside when you need to wake up.

- Another trick is to set your alarm clock on the other side of the room. You will actually have to get out of bed to turn it off, and then guess what? You're awake!
- A funny way to wake up is to use a Clocky alarm clock. This is a silly alarm clock that runs away from you so that you have to chase it around the room to catch it and turn it off.
- In the spring and summer, try leaving your shades open to let natural light in in the morning.
- Your parents might be willing to give you a "ten-minute warning" and a "five-minute warning" to wake you up gradually before you absolutely have to get out of bed. Talk to your parents and figure out what works best for you.

Prepare the Night Before

So now that you have some ideas of how to get out of bed on time, let's talk about the rest of your morning routine. Remember that a good morning starts the night before!

Each night before you go to bed, lay out what you're going to wear in the morning and put everything you need to take to school in your backpack. If you need your mom or dad to sign a paper, make sure to do that the night before. If you make your own lunch, you could also try getting most of your lunch ready the night before. The more you can get done the night before, the easier your mornings will be!

Create a "Launching Pad"

Create a "launching pad"—a particular place where you put everything you need for school. Gather everything you will need for school the next day, and put it on your launching pad the night before. Do you need your musical instrument? Your soccer cleats? Money for the school field trip? Think about what's happening tomorrow and ask your mom or dad for help to remember if there is anything special you will need. Put everything on your launching pad. You'll be all set to have a good day.

Stay on Track

When you have AD/HD, it's easy to get distracted and get off the track of your morning routine.

For example, if your brother or sister is getting ready for school at the same time, you might start talking to them and stop getting dressed. Or you might see something in your room and start playing with it.

One boy with AD/HD solved this problem by bringing his clothes downstairs to the powder room near the kitchen where his dad was preparing his breakfast. That way he didn't get distracted by things in his room and his dad was nearby to help keep him on track and aware of what time it was.

Do you think this strategy might work for you?

Reward Yourself!

It's hard work changing old habits and developing new ones. Set a reward with your mom or dad. For example, some kids really like it if they get to watch TV or play for a few minutes if they get ready quickly and have a few minutes before they have to leave for school.

Time for a Break!

Can you spot the differences between these two pictures? (Hint: there are seven differences!)

CHAPTER FOUR

Your After-School Routine

YOUR afternoon routine may be more complicated than your morning routine, because you probably don't do the same thing after school each day.

You may have a lesson or a sports practice on some afternoons and come straight home from school on other afternoons.

Other kids are in after-care at school and don't come home until supper time.

The afternoon routine discussed in this chapter is for afternoons when you come straight home after school.

If you stay at school in after-care, then you'll need to create a routine there so that you have time to relax, get some exercise, and get your homework done, too.

Create an After-School Routine

First, make a list of things you need to do after school every day. Talk to your mom or dad about what things need to go in your after-school routine.

Make sure you leave yourself enough time to get everything done. It may help to work backwards from dinnertime.

For example, your list might look something like this:

- Snack – 20 minutes

- Chill time – a good time to get reading done or do something active outside – 30 minutes

- Practice the flute – 20 minutes

- Homework – 1 hour

- Help with dinner and setting the table – 20 minutes

What does your after-school routine look like? Talk to your mom or dad about what your routine should be on afternoons when you don't come straight home from school. Maybe you won't have time to practice a musical instrument or help with dinner on afternoons when you have a lesson or sports practice after school.

My After-School Routine

Write the steps off on the left-hand side. Then check them off each school day. Your steps can include things like: eat a snack, go outside, do my homework, feed the dog, practice my instrument, or other things you think of with your mom or dad.

Steps	Mon	Tues	Wed	Thu	Fri
1					
2					
3					
4					
5					
6					

Build in Breaks

Notice that the sample routine on page 43 includes breaks for a snack and reading and then flute practice before homework time.

That's because your brain needs a break after being in school all day.

Watch out for Digital Distractions

What gets in the way of doing your after-school routine?

Do you sometimes start watching TV or playing a video game instead of starting your homework?

Some families have declared their home to be a "digital-free zone" on school nights so there's no risk of spending time on your phone or iPad or watching TV when you need to be doing homework or keeping up with assigned reading.

Time for a Break!

Can you help Maddie avoid distractions and find her way to the "digital-free zone"?

CHAPTER FIVE

Your Bedtime Routine

YOUR bedtime routine is one of the most important routines of the day because following a good bedtime routine will ensure that you'll get a good night's sleep. Did you know that getting enough sleep every night is the most important thing you can do to help your brain to learn, remember, plan, and be organized? And when you are in elementary school, your body needs 10 or 11 hours of sleep every night.

Make Sure You Get Enough Sleep

If you're not getting to bed early enough to get 10 hours of sleep, it's important to figure out what needs to change. Here are a few things that might be interfering with sleep:

Evening Activities

Today's busy families often go out and do activities in the evening. For example, scout troops may meet in the evening because the parent running the group works full time. Some sports have evening practice sessions. And sometimes lessons and other activities are scheduled in the evening because parents aren't home in the afternoon to take you to earlier lessons. You need to talk about evening activities with your parents and decide whether you're involved in too many activities that are interfering with getting enough sleep. We know it's hard to give up activities that you like, but it's even harder to go through your days always feeling tired and not having enough energy to focus and learn and get your homework done.

Screen Time

If you're like a lot of other kids, it's "screen time" that gets in the way of bedtime. By screen time we mean time spent in front of your TV, iPad, computer, or phone. The best way to make sure that screen time isn't robbing you of sleep is to turn in all of your digital devices to your parents before you start your bedtime routine. That way you won't be tempted to get on your iPad or phone after bedtime.

Not Paying Attention to What Time It Is

It's easy in a busy family to lose track of what time it is. Your mom or dad are busy preparing dinner and cleaning up after dinner, doing laundry, helping with homework, and lots of other things. So it's easy for them, and for you, to lose track of time and not start getting ready for bed on time.

Not Starting Your Homework Early Enough

Remember the sample after-school routine in the last chapter? It included breaks for a snack and reading, then flute practice for 20 minutes, and then starting homework.

If you have a lesson or sports practice after school, you'll need to start on your homework as soon as you get home.

Your mom and dad can help you do this by creating a "digital-free zone" on school nights so that you're not tempted by the TV, computer, tablet, or phone.

Create a Bedtime Routine

Now, it's time for you and your mom or dad to sit down and write down your bedtime routine.

Keep your bedtime routine posted in your bedroom where you'll see it while you go through your routine.

Your routine may look something like this:

7:00 PM	Put things in my backpack for tomorrow. Be sure to put my homework in the homework folder.
	Turn in electronics! Give mom or dad my electronic devices (like my phone and iPad). This way I won't be tempted to start using them after bedtime.
7:15 PM	Take shower
	Brush teeth
	Put on PJ's
7:45 PM	Lay out clothes for tomorrow
8:00 PM	Get in bed and read
8:30 PM	Lights out

Your routine may be different on certain days, for example if you have sports practice and get home later. If you have lessons or practices on certain days, you may want to write a routine that fits each school day instead of one routine that's the same every day.

My Bedtime Routine

You can use the bedtime routine in the book as a guide to developing your own personal bedtime routine. We've included the most important parts of a good bedtime routine on the list and left a few blank spaces for you to add other things to your bedtime routine.

Bedtime Routine	Mon	Tue	Wed	Thu	Fri
1 Turn in all digital devices					
2					
3					
4					
5					
6 In bed doing quiet non-screen-based activity					
7 Lights out at _____ PM					

Falling Asleep

Here are some tips if you have difficulty falling asleep after you go to bed:

- Don't sleep late on Sunday! That makes it hard to fall asleep by 8:30 Sunday night and sets you up to feel tired the next day.
- Give yourself some quiet time in bed before lights out. Read or listen to soft music for 20-30 minutes.
- Don't use electronics after bedtime. Turn in your digital devices so you won't be tempted to use them.
- Make sure your homework is done so you're not worrying about it.

Good luck! We know you'll be feeling rested in the morning as soon as you practice your routine until it becomes a habit!

Remember:
- Start slowly—pick one routine to work on until you master it.
- Problem solve with your parents if something isn't working in your routine.
- Use a checklist until each step becomes automatic.
- And don't give up—practice makes perfect.

Time for a Break!

Can you unscramble the words below? Hint: they are all related to bedtime!

ELEPS   — — — — —

MERDA   — — — — —

ZOESON   — — — — — —

XERLA   — — — — —

STER   — — — —

SLEEP   REST   DREAM
RELAX   SNOOZE

CHAPTER SIX

Organizing Your Stuff

IF you're like lots of other kids, keeping your room organized and all of your things organized is not easy. And it can be even harder when you have AD/HD!

Have you ever cleaned up your room only to discover the next day it looks as if you'd never cleaned it up? In this chapter, we'll give you lots of tips on getting your room and your things in order—and keeping them in order—so that you can find what you need.

The Clutter Problem

There are two common reasons why kids' rooms are disorganized: having too much stuff, and having nowhere to put it.

Too Much Stuff!

Have you saved all of your stuffed animals from when you were little? Do you have lots of games with missing pieces that you never play with? Maybe your drawers and closets are stuffed with things that don't fit you any more. If so, you've got too much stuff!

Having too much stuff is part of the clutter problem—part of why your room, backpack, and desk are all cluttered. In this chapter, we'll teach you what to do when you have too much stuff.

Nowhere to Put It!

Another part of the clutter problem is having nowhere to put all of your stuff. Do you just move things from one place to another without being able to put them away? For example, do you clear off your bed by putting things on the floor or on top of your dresser? Or maybe you need to clear off your desk, so you pile lots of things on your bed. When you don't have enough storage, you just shift your clutter from one place to another without being able to really make things neat and orderly.

Do a Bedroom "Dig-Out"

You can tackle your clutter problem by doing a bedroom "dig-out." The first time you dig out your room, you'll probably need help from your mom or dad. They should be there to help you and give you advice, but not to do it for you. A big part of de-cluttering your room is deciding where you want your furniture and where you want to store your things.

Talk to your mom or dad about your room dig-out. They probably have some ideas about how much stuff you need to clear out of your room and whether you need more storage space.

Make a plan and include breaks so that you and your parent don't get too tired and not want to finish reorganizing your room.

Start with four big plastic bins or cardboard boxes. Label your four bins with big, easy-to-read labels. Writing with a marker on wide masking tape is an easy way to label your bins and be able to read the labels from across the room. Label your four bins:

- Give away
- Throw away
- Stow away
- Keep

Give Away

Giveaways are things that someone else might want to use that you don't use any more. You might give things away to a younger brother or sister (such as clothes that are too small or toys that are for younger kids), and you might want to give some other things away to a local charity. It helps to make a rule about what you're going to give away. One rule that might work for you is:

If I haven't used it in a year, give it to someone that *will* use it.

Throw Away

Throwaways are things that no one can really use, like trash, old papers, broken toys, games with missing pieces, and clothing that is torn or stained.

Stow Away

Stowaway items are things that you aren't using right now, but may want to use later. Things like:

- Out of season clothing. For example, during the summer months, you would stow away your winter coats, boots, and snow suits. In the cold months, you would stow away things like bathing suits, beach towels, shorts, and sleeveless shirts.

- Equipment you're not using right now but may use later. You might have sports equipment, but you're not playing that sport right now, or you may have a musical instrument and music stand, but you've stopped taking lessons for now.

- Things you're attached to, but don't want cluttering your room—these might include favorite books, games, or stuffed animals that you are attached to, but don't really play with any longer.

Keep

Deciding on the items that go in your "keep" bin may seem easy, but you may need to do a lot of talking with your mom or dad about what you really want to keep in your room. For example, you might have too many of something and not really have room to kccp it all in your room.

Finding a Home for Your "Keepers"

Once you've decided, with your parents, what you're going to keep in your room, it's time to give all of your keepers a home. It's so much easier to keep your room neat if there is a special place where each of your belongings lives. So the next step is to decide whether you have enough storage and the right kind of storage.

Clothes Storage

Do you have enough room in your closet and dresser drawers? Do you have an organized way to store your shoes so that you can find them? You need to clear out your dresser and closet enough that you have room for all of your clothes—that is, the clothes that you wear right now. If you don't have room for clothes for other seasons of the year, that's okay. You can store your out-of-season clothes in a "stowaway bin." Label the bin, and then switch clothes from the stowaway bin and closet as the season changes.

Stuff Storage

Different kids have different kinds of things that they want to keep in their room.

You might want to keep lots of Legos in your room, or lots of books or stuffed animals. You might have pet turtles or fish in your room.

Whatever you keep in your room, you'll need to be sure that you have enough shelves and places to store your things so that they each have their own "home" and aren't just kept in a jumble.

Storage doesn't have to be expensive. If you have collections of things that you want to keep in your room and take out to play with sometimes, you might want to get some clear plastic bins (so you know what's inside) that are the right size to shove under your bed.

Keeping Your Room Organized

Congratulations! You've cleaned up and organized your room.

Now comes the tricky part. If you keep doing the same things you did before, your room will be messy in no time at all.

So here are the things you need to practice to keep your room neat and organized:

- If you take it out, put it back. This will be much easier because everything in your room has a home now.

- If you wear it, hang it back up or put it in the laundry basket if it's dirty. You could try changing clothes near your closet and your laundry basket. That way, it's super easy to hang things up or put them in the laundry.

- When you add something, always subtract something. Your room will never be a big crowded mess again if you do one simple thing. Whenever you bring something new into your room, you need to take something out that's the same size. Decide if the item you're subtracting is a throwaway, giveaway, or stowaway (if you want to use it later).

- Every season—spring, summer, fall and winter—do a dig-out in your room, getting rid of things you no longer use and making sure that everything you keep has a nice home. Now that you've done the "big dig" you'll find that your seasonal dig-outs go very quickly and you'll enjoy your organized room.

Time for a Break!

Can you find the food items hidden in the picture below? (Hint: take a look at the answer key at the bottom of the page!)

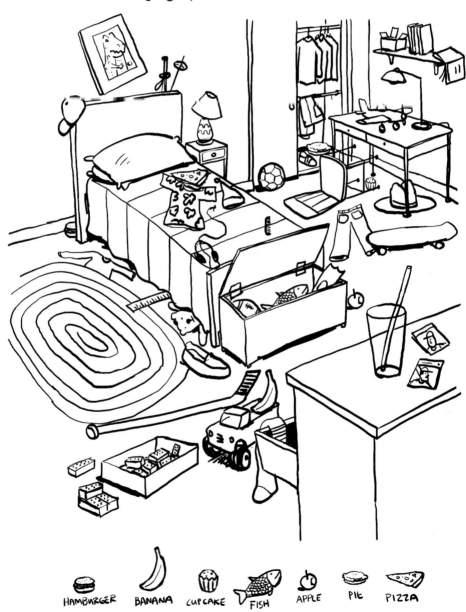

HAMBURGER   BANANA   CUPCAKE   FISH   APPLE   PIE   PIZZA

CHAPTER SEVEN

Learning How to Get Things Done

ONE of the most important things that you can learn is how to get things done.

Life is full of lots of things that are really important to do that don't feel like fun—things like chores and homework, for example. And when you don't feel like doing something, what do you usually do? If you're like lots of other kids (and grown-ups too) what you do is procrastinate. You tell yourself, "I'll do it later," or "I don't need to do it now, it's not due until Monday." And you keep putting things off until there's a crisis.

In this chapter, we're going to give you some ideas about how to make it easier and more fun to get things done.

Make an Appointment With Yourself

Did you know that you're more likely to get things done if you have scheduled a specific day and time to do them? It's true! If you don't have a specific time to do homework or to do chores, you'll keep putting it off because there will always seem to be time to do it "later" instead of "now."

But when you have scheduled a time on your agenda or calendar, when that time comes, you're less likely to do something else.

You're also more likely to do things if you schedule them for the same time each day or each week, like always emptying the dishwasher when you get home from school or always cleaning up your room on Saturday morning before you go off to do something else.

Talk to your mom or dad about good times to schedule your chores and homework, then write them down on your agenda or calendar.

Look for Ways to Make It Fun!

Here are some ideas for ways to make it more fun to do your chores. We bet you can come up with some other good ideas too.

Listen to fast, energetic music that you like.
Fast music with a good beat makes everyone feel more energetic. Our bodies naturally want to move when we hear good dance music—that's why so many people listen to dance music when they exercise at the gym. It makes it easier to move and keep going. So next time you need to clean up your room or pick up your toys, turn on the music and move!

Turn it into a competition.
Some kids are more motivated when there is a competition. For example, if you have a brother or sister, you can set up a competition that whoever completes their chores for the day or for the week first wins a prize. You'll need to talk to your parents about how to set up this competition so that it's fair and everyone understands the rules. You could also set up a second prize for the runner-up if they complete all of their chores before a certain time. The important thing is to help motivate you and your siblings to get things done.

Play "beat the clock."
If there's no one else to compete with, play "beat the clock" with yourself. Time how long it takes you

to do a particular chore. Then the next time you do it, play "beat the clock": set a timer for the number of minutes it took you last time and see if you can do it a little faster this time. Playing "beat the clock" will help you stay focused on your task instead of starting to do something else that catches your eye. But remember, playing "beat the clock" doesn't mean doing a bad job of your chore just so you can do it more quickly! It means doing a good job in a more efficient way.

Turn it into a pretend game.
Use your imagination to turn your task into a pretend game. For example, did you know that students at West Point or the Naval Academy (colleges where students are trained to become army or navy officers) have very tough room inspections? Some say that room inspections are one of the most difficult things to pass. Their beds have to be made perfectly, with sheets tucked in so tight that you can bounce a coin on the surface. And every item of clothing has to be folded in a specific way and put into a specific drawer.

It could be fun to pretend that you were an army cadet or navy midshipman getting ready for room inspection. Look around your room and see if you can make everything perfect. Make your bed carefully, hang up your clothes carefully, line up your shoes in the closet, and straighten up your desk and shelves so that you can "pass inspection."

Get other people to help out.

Sometimes, it can be more fun if you do the chore with someone else. That's what the saying "Many hands make light work" means. When you have many hands working on the same task, it gets done much more quickly. Offer to help out with other chores in exchange for help with yours. For example, you could offer to help your mom or dad clean up the kitchen, and they could help you clean up your room. Or you could help your brother or sister clean their room and then they could help you clean yours.

Save the best for last.
Often, we put off doing a chore or a homework assignment because we're involved in doing something we enjoy and don't want to stop.

Pulling yourself away from something fun to do something that's not so much fun is doing it the hard way.

Instead, make a rule to "save the best for last." In other words, reward yourself for a job well done by doing one of your favorite activities.

That way you'll be motivated to finish your chore or your assignment because you are looking forward to doing something fun.

Can you think of other ways to make a chore fun? Think of the chore or task that is your least favorite and then try one of the ways we've suggested, to make the time go by more quickly while you do the task.

Which one do you think would work best for you?

Try one approach this week and then try another one next week. Pretty soon you'll be much better at making the time fly by while you're doing chores.

Divide and Conquer

"Divide and conquer" means dividing something that is hard to do into smaller parts so you can "conquer" the task and get it done more easily. When you have a lot to do, sometimes the best way to get it done is to divide and conquer. It's much easier to begin a small task than a large one. And when it's small, you can go all the way to the end and have the satisfaction of finishing the job.

For example, if you are trying to clean up your room, you could divide it into smaller steps such as:

 Pick up clothes on the floor and put them into the laundry hamper.

 Put books back onto the book shelf.

 Put your toys back into their storage containers.

 Put your your stuffed animals where they belong.

Do you feel like you have too much to do between after school activities, chores, and homework? Sit down with your mom and dad and make a list of the chores that you need to do to help keep your house in order. Are there any that you can break up into smaller parts?

Then, sit down with your mom or dad and make a schedule. Write on your weekly calendar when you will do each part so that all of your chores will be done by lunch time on Saturday. We bet you'll see that with a little planning, and dividing your chores up into smaller tasks, your chores won't take very long at all.

So remember, to get things done:

 Make an appointment with yourself and write it on your calendar.

 Look for ways to make it fun.

 Divide and conquer—turn one big task into a few small tasks.

Try these strategies and we bet you'll find that it's much easier to keep up with everything you need to get done!

Time for a Break!

Maddie needs to put all her clothes in the laundry basket, but she's having trouble finding one of her socks. Can you help her find it?

CHAPTER EIGHT

Managing Your Time

WHEN you're little, your parents and your teachers keep track of time for you. Your parents tell you when it's time to get up, when to leave for school, when to start your homework, and when to go to bed. At school, your teacher keeps track of the time, telling the class when to start an assignment, when to leave for another classroom, and when to go to lunch.

Now that you're getting a little older, it's time for you to start paying attention to time. In this chapter, you'll read about all sorts of different tools that can help you keep track of what time it is. You will also learn about how to keep track of the passage of time—how long you are spending doing something. We'll talk about using calendars to keep track of the days and weeks and plan ahead for assignments and activities. There's lots to learn, but you don't need to learn it all at once.

Keeping Track of What Time It Is

The first task as you're learning to manage your time is to notice what time it is. The tools for this job are clocks and watches. You can also use a smart phone, if you have one. It's easiest if you have digital clocks and watches—that is, clocks and watches that show numbers instead of clocks and watches that have hour hands and minute hands.

If you don't already have one, ask your mom or dad if you can have a clock in your bedroom with large numbers on it so that you can easily read it from across the room.

But it's a good habit to start carrying something with you all the time that can tell you what time it is—either a watch on your arm or a phone in your pocket. A watch is often the best idea because it's less expensive, harder to lose, and you're allowed to have a watch with you in the classroom.

There are watches that can be very helpful that vibrate and will give you a text message to remind you what you're supposed to be doing. Two of these watches are the WatchMinder and the Cadex 12-alarm watch. Talk with your parents to decide if one of these watches would help you to keep track of time and what you're supposed to be doing.

Some kids with AD/HD have a harder time keeping track of time. Even if they have a clock in their room or a watch on their arm, they may forget to look at them to check the time. Kids that forget to check the time are always running late, which is stressful for them and for their parents.

If you forget to check the time, here are a couple of things to try:

Use a Time Timer.
A Time Timer is a timer that has a big round face with no numbers on it. You can set the Time Timer for as many minutes as you like, up to an hour. The time that you have left shows up in bright red on the clock face and the red portion gets smaller and smaller as it gets closer to the time. If you have a Time Timer in your bedroom and another at the kitchen table, you'll be more likely to know how much time you have left.

Schedule reminders on your phone.
Some kids program their phones so that there is an alarm that goes off when it's time to get up, another one that goes off when it's time to eat breakfast, and a third alarm that goes off when it's time to leave for school. A smart way to schedule the alarms is to have them go off five minutes before you need to do the next thing. That way, you have a five-minute warning and can stay on time during your morning routine.

Get in the habit of setting reminders.
Whether you use a watch with reminders that can be set (like a Watchminder or Cadex 12-alarm watch), or a phone, it's a great habit to get into to set alarms that remind you when to end an activity and start the next one. For example, setting a reminder will help a lot if your mom or dad says you can play outside for an hour before you come in to start your homework. That way, you can be responsible for knowing when to come inside, and your parents won't have to remind you.

Keeping Track of Days and Weeks
We've been talking about hours and minutes so far, but we also measure time in days, weeks, months and years. That's what calendars are for.

Use a family calendar.

If you're in kindergarten or first grade, you've learned about the days of the week. You've learned that every seven days the week starts all over again. And you know that Monday through Friday are school days, while Saturday and Sunday are weekend days when you don't go to school.

One type of calendar that can be very helpful for kindergarten and first-grade kids is a big dry-erase "family calendar" where you and your parents can write down what's happening on each day. Your family can keep it in the kitchen or family room—wherever everyone will see it.

Use a personal calendar.

When you're a little older, it's time to start learning to keep your own personal calendar, or agenda. You may still have a family calendar in the kitchen, but you also need one for yourself. Your personal calendar is a place to write down everything you need to remember for the week, including:

- Homework assignments
- Dates of tests
- After-school sports, activities, or lessons
- Play dates and birthday parties
- Appointments your parents have made for you with the dentist or doctor

My Week

SUNDAY	go to game with Sara ☺
MONDAY	Spelling test
TUESDAY	take flute to school
WEDNESDAY	bring permission slip for field trip tomorrow
THURSDAY	Field trip! Bring $3.00 for picnic lunch
FRIDAY	
SATURDAY	

Once you have an agenda, keep it with you always. It's best to get one that is hole-punched so that it can be kept in your binder. Then, every night, sit with your mom and dad and take a few minutes to plan for the next day as well as to write in new assignments or events that you need to keep track of.

And be sure to plan ahead on your agenda. For example, if you have a book report due next week, you can use your agenda to plan for it and keep yourself on track. You might plan to read the book for a half-hour every day this week and then write the book report over the weekend.

Estimating Time

There's another very important aspect of learning to manage your time: estimating how long things take. If you don't know how long it takes you to walk to the bus stop, you don't know when to leave the house.

If you don't know how long it will take to finish your math homework, then it's hard to plan your other activities.

Getting good at estimating time takes practice. Most people think that things can be done more quickly than they really can.

With your mom or dad, practice estimating how long things take and see if you can get better and better at it.

For example, estimate how long it takes you to go through your whole bedtime routine including taking a shower, brushing your teeth, getting into your pajamas, putting out your clothes for tomorrow, and getting in bed.

Write down how long you think it takes, then set a timer and see how accurate you are. Don't rush! You're not playing "beat the clock." You're trying to figure out how long it really takes on a normal night. That way, you'll know when you need to start getting ready in order to be in bed on time.

Try estimating other things too, like how long your reading assignment will take, how long your math homework will take, and how long it takes you to walk the dog.

Make a time estimation chart and see if you can become more and more accurate in knowing how long things really take.

The more accurate you are, the better you'll be able to manage your time.

Planning for Unexpected Things

Another part of managing your time well is to leave some extra time in case things don't happen according to your plan.

For example, it might only take you four minutes to walk to your school bus stop. But if you only leave four minutes, then you'll miss the bus if something happens—like if your dog runs out the gate and follows you, or you suddenly realize you left your lunch box on the kitchen counter.

Good time managers always leave a little time for the unexpected.

Becoming a Good Time Manager

We've talked about a lot of different skills in this chapter. You don't need to learn them all at once.

By the time you are in third grade you should be in the habit of checking a calendar to know what is coming up, and by the time you're ready for middle school, you should set a goal of using an agenda regularly to keep track of assignments.

You'll have a much easier time as you go through the higher grades if you develop good time management skills now. So start small and keep building good habits:

- Pay attention to what time it is.
- Set reminders so that you can get up and get ready in the morning.
- Use a Time Timer or other sort of timer to keep track of how long you've been doing an activity.
- Pay attention to what day it is and what's happening each day.
- Write future events on a calendar.
- Start to use an agenda to keep track of daily and future assignments.
- Learn to estimate how long things take.
- Learn to leave extra time for unexpected things.

If you learn all of these things in elementary school you'll be in great shape to start middle school and be able to comfortably keep track of all of your classes, assignments, and activities.

Time for a Break!

Connect the dots!

CHAPTER NINE

Planning a Project

HAVE you ever planned a project before? A project can seem complicated at first, but once you figure out how to do it, you'll be able to complete projects more and more easily. Some projects are assigned at school, like a science project. Other projects are things you'd like to do at home, like redecorating your room.

Making cookies is a simple and fun project. First, you need to plan your project to decide when you are going to make the cookies—make sure you plan a time when your mom or dad can help.

Think about all of the ingredients you'll need for your cookies. Look at the recipe with your mom or dad to make sure you have all of the ingredients.

Then think about the steps to making cookies. You need to turn on the oven and wait for it to heat up to the right temperature. You need to follow the steps of the recipe to mix up all of the ingredients in the right order. Lastly, you need to put the cookie dough out on the baking sheets and then put them in the oven.

Now it's time to be patient! Set the timer and then wait for the timer to go off. Get help from your mom or dad when taking the cookies out of the oven—be careful! It's hot!

If this is your first time making cookies, they may not come out just right. They may fall apart, or be too hard. Don't worry. Be persistent and problem solve. Maybe the oven was too hot. Maybe you forgot to mix in the egg. If things don't go right, figure out what needs to change, and next time you'll be successful. And the best reward for your successful project is that you get to eat the cookies. **Yum!**

There are five steps to completing a project—
the same steps you read about above for baking
cookies. Let's think about them one at a time.
We call them the Five Ps of completing a project
successfully.

Let's think about a fun project like redecorating
a wall of your bedroom and see how the Five Ps
work.

Planning. If you want to redecorate your
wall, you'll need to plan what you'll need.
For example, you might need paint, stencils
or decals, and maybe posters of your favorite sports
star, superhero, or singer. You'll need to choose the
color of paint. Your mom or dad or another adult will
need to paint the wall for you, so it's important to
find a time when they can help you.

Preparation. After you make your plan, it's
time to prepare for your project. You need
to get everything together that you'll need
for your project—for example, paint, paint brushes
and rollers, and drop cloths to protect the floor. You
may need to move furniture out of the way. Gather
together all of the wall decorations you've planned.
Now, schedule each step. You'll need to let the
paint dry, and you will probably need more than
one coat of paint to cover over the paint that's on
your wall now. Once you've done the planning and
preparation, you're ready to begin.

Patience. Having patience is an important ingredient in every project. Remember not to rush through your project. Give yourself time to think about and follow your plan. For example, being patient means letting the paint dry before you move on to the next step. Being patient means doing things carefully so you are less likely to make mistakes. Make sure you've measured exactly where to hang your posters or decals Take your time.

 Persistence. Being persistent means sticking with your project if it is taking longer. Persistence also means not giving up when things don't go as planned. For example, your dad may have a change of plans that means you'll have to wait until next weekend to paint your wall. Or your favorite poster may get wrinkled or torn accidentally.

 Problem solving. Don't worry if you run into a problem as you work on your project. Running into a problem just means that it's time for problem solving. Even the best-planned projects can run into problems. For example, if one of your posters is wrinkled or torn, you can try to repair it, or choose something else for your wall decoration.

Follow these five steps every time and you'll have successful projects and a beautiful new wall in your bedroom!

Planning a Simple Project

Name of my project:

List of supplies I need for my project:

1 _____

2 _____

3 _____

4 _____

5 _____

List each task you need to do and how long each task will take:

Task	How long?
1	
2	
3	
4	
5	

Decide when you are going to do each task. If your project has a deadline, such as a school project, make sure that your last task is scheduled well BEFORE the deadline. Leave some extra time in case something goes wrong and you have to do it over. And remember, some projects require you to wait between tasks—for example, if glue needs to dry, or if something you are cooking needs time to bake.

Day	Time	Will I need help?
Task 1		
Task 2		
Task 3		
Task 4		
Task 5		

Remember, if you need help on a task, you'll need to check with your mom or dad or another helper to find out when they can help you.

Terrific! Just follow these three steps and you'll always be a great project planner!

Time for a Break!

Imagine you were planning a project to decorate one of your walls. How would you decorate it? Draw a picture of it here:

CHAPTER TEN

Ways to Remember

IF you're like lots of other kids, it's hard to remember everything you need to. And if you have AD/HD, remembering is even harder! There are lots of different kinds of memory. You can be good at some kinds of remembering and have a hard time with other kinds. So, let's start off with a little quiz about remembering. Why don't you take this quiz with your mom or dad so that you can see if they see things the same way that you do.

Remembering and Forgetting Quiz

Please answer each question with the number that best describes you:

1: a little like me

2: somewhat like me

3: very much like me

____ It's hard for me to remember my teacher's instructions.

____ Sometimes I forget information a friend has told me.

____ I forget to bring things home from school at the end of the day.

____ It's hard for me to remember things that my parents have asked me to do.

___ It's hard for me to remember to do something later.

___ It's hard to remember to bring everything I need for school each day.

___ It's hard for me to remember where I put things.

___ It's hard for me to remember future events—like when a project is due or when a school event will take place.

___ It's hard for me to remember the details of what happened a few days ago.

___ It's hard for me to remember the details about something I have read.

___ It's hard for me to remember to do all the steps of my daily routines.

___ It's hard for me to remember my weekly schedule—like what day I have soccer practice and what day I have my music lesson.

Do you and your parents agree about the things that you have trouble remembering? Sometimes, people around us have a clearer view of our behavior than we do. What are the main areas that you have difficulty remembering?

In this chapter, we'll talk about different ways to remind yourself of things that are important to remember. Lots of kids use their mom or dad as their reminder system. But if they are the reminders all the time, you'll never learn how to remind yourself! So here are some things that can help you remember. And if one kind of reminder doesn't work, don't feel discouraged. That just means that you need to think of a different way to remind yourself that works for you. We're going to teach you about a lot of different ways to remind yourself. Your job is to experiment and see which way works best for you. Probably, you'll need to use different types of reminders for different things that you tend to forget.

Ways to Remind Yourself

Here are some common things that kids have trouble remembering, and some ideas for ways to remember them. Do you think any of these solutions would work for you?

Problem: not remembering to put things away.
Do you ever have trouble remembering to put your things away, like hanging up your jacket when you come home, putting your dirty clothes in the hamper, or putting your books and homework into your backpack each night?

Solution: make it a habit to "tie the bow."
The "putting things away" habit is one of the
most important habits you can learn. When you
always put things away *where they belong* then
you'll always know where to find them when
you need them.

Putting things where they belong means that each
thing needs a "home"—a special place where it
goes. Remember the chapter about digging out
and re-organizing your room? After you organize
your room, you should have a special place where
everything belongs.

So now, comes the "putting things away" habit. We
call it "tying the bow" because the last thing you do
when you're wrapping a package is "tie the bow."
Just like when you're doing something, the last step
is to put things you've used away—to "tie the bow"
on your activity. If you think about it, clutter comes
from forgetting to tie the bow over and over again.

Look around your room right now and see how many "bows" you've forgotten to tie. Your untied bows might look something like this:

- shoes in the middle of the floor

- clothes dropped on the floor

- toys left out on your bed or on the floor

- homework and school books left wherever you were using them

Remember reading about building habits in Chapter 2? You can build a habit of "tying the bow" by tying the new habit to a habit you already have: for example, hanging up your jacket and putting away your shoes as soon as you get home, or putting your books and homework back in your backpack each night when you finish your homework. The more you think about putting things where they belong, the easier it will become to "tie the bow" each time.

Why don't you and your parents see how quickly you can remember to "tie the bow" and put things where they go? Sometimes it can help to keep track of your "bow tying" by making a chart of the things you're trying to remember to complete or put away each day and going over the chart with your parents. We bet you'll see more and more check marks on your bow-tying chart as time goes by. And if there are certain things you continue to forget to put away, then it's time for some problem-solving with your parents. For example, creating a big reminder for yourself, or finding a more convenient place to put a specific belonging if you keep forgetting.

Problem: Forgetting to tell your mom or dad something important.

For example, maybe your friend's mom calls to say that your Cub Scout meeting is going to start early this week and you need to be sure to get there on time. Do you sometimes answer the phone, but then don't write down an important message like this?

Solution: Write a sticky note reminder.

Keep a pad of sticky notes in your backpack and write yourself a note reminder.

Stick the reminder where you'll be sure to see it later.

If you write a reminder note at school, you can stick it on the first page of your binder so you'll see it when you open it to do homework.

If you're home when you write the note, stick the note on the kitchen counter or somewhere else your mom or dad will be sure to see it.

Don't try to keep it in your head! Remember, a short note is better than a long memory.

Problem: Forgetting to do chores or homework without a reminder.

If you're like a lot of kids, you don't get up in the morning thinking about everything you need to do. You're used to your mom or dad or teacher reminding you throughout the day what you need to do next. But this doesn't work when there are no adults around to remind you. Also, your parents want to help you become more independent so that they don't have to remind you all the time. So, what can you do to remember to do your chores or to start your homework?

Solution: Build a habit and create a reminder.

First, build a habit. It's easier to remember to do things if you do them at the same time each day, in the same order. Chores and homework fall into your after-school routine, so go back to Chapter 4 to review how to build a good after-school routine. The main idea to keep in mind is to save the activities you like as a reward for completing the activities you need to do, but may not enjoy, like chores or homework. Once you start watching TV or playing games on your computer or your iPad, you are almost certain to forget to stop and do your chores and homework, so save the fun stuff for later and you'll get your chores and homework done.

Second, build in reminders. if you have a watch that gives reminders you can program reminders to go off at the times that you're supposed to do your chores or start on your homework. And if you don't have a reminder watch, you can always use a kitchen timer.

Problem: Forgetting to take things you need to school.

Do you ever forget your athletic gear on days when you have practice, or your musical instrument on days you have a lesson after school?

Solution: Put it on your "launch pad."

Your "launch pad" is the place where you gather things you need to take with you to school—a paper signed by your parents, a library book, soccer cleats, a musical instrument, as well as your backpack and lunch box.

Get in the habit of putting things on your launch pad the moment you think of it.

If it's hard for you to remember what you need each day of the week, ask your mom or dad to help you create a launch pad list for each day of the week, and post it on the wall beside your launch pad. That way, as you're getting ready to leave for school, just check your launch pad list for the day to make sure you've got what you need.

Remember—a short checklist is better than a long memory!

Problem: Forgetting to bring things home from school or other places.

Do you sometimes forget to bring home your jacket or umbrella or something else you took to school or to a friend's house?

Solution: Put everything in your backpack.

If you're like most kids, your backpack is the one thing you're used to taking with you whenever you to go school or to a friend's house or another activity after school. The same thing can work for athletic gear: always put your cleats, shin guards, helmet, and whatever else you might need in your athletic bag because you're much less likely to forget your bag or your backpack. So remember:

Pack things inside to take them along for the ride!

Problem: Forgetting about future events.
Do you sometimes forget to ask your parents to buy materials for a school project? Or forget when picture day is at school? Or forget when you need to take a check and permission form to school for the field trip? As you get older you will have more and more future events that you need to remember. And your mom and dad can't always be there to remind you, so now's a good time to learn how to remind yourself.

Solution: Use a calendar as your reminder.
First, you'll need to get in the habit of writing things down on your personal calendar. It's a good idea to keep your calendar in a central place where you and your parents can easily see it and you can add things to it.

Ask your parents to get you a calendar with big squares on it so that have room to write what you want to remember. Then sit down with them and write down the things you need to remember over the next month.

A calendar won't help you remember if you don't have the habit of checking your calendar. So work with your mom or dad to check your calendar every evening. Right after finishing your homework might be a good time. This is also a time to think about new things to write on your calendar. For example, maybe you've been invited to a birthday party. So write that date on the calendar and write on your calendar a few days earlier to buy a gift and birthday card!

So, you see, there are lots of ways to remind yourself:

1. Build a habit of "tying the bow."

2. Write a sticky note.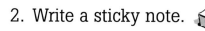

3. Build a habit to do it at the same time of day or week and set an alarm reminder.

4. Put it on your launch pad.

5. Put it inside something you'll remember (backpack or athletic bag).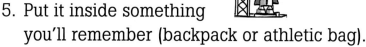

6. Put it on your calendar.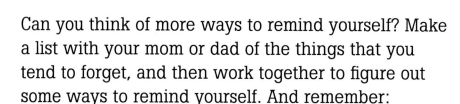

Can you think of more ways to remind yourself? Make a list with your mom or dad of the things that you tend to forget, and then work together to figure out some ways to remind yourself. And remember:

Reminders work better than trying to keep things in your head!

Even if you're *sure* you'll remember something, create a reminder anyway.

We've talked about a lot of different ways to help yourself remember what you need to do. Don't try to do all of these at once. Each type of reminder requires building a habit, so pick one type of reminder and work with your mom or dad until you're using that reminder very regularly. Then move on to another one.

Good luck! I think you'll soon find that you're remembering things much better.

Time for a Break!

Unscramble the three words below and fill in the blanks to reveal the secret message!

AMESOWE
LNAP
GNORAZIED

_____ job! Now you know all about how to _____ and be _____! Keep up the good work!

CONGRATULATIONS! You've learned about a lot of different planning and organizing skills in this book. I hope you've had fun, and learned a lot, too.

The skills you have learned about in this book will help you for the rest of your life! It's important for you and your parents to remember that learning these skills is something that you should work on throughout your elementary school years. Don't try to do them all at once!

Talk to your mom or dad and decide on what you'll start practicing first. Give yourself plenty of time to practice your new skill before you add another one. The longer you practice, the easier it will become.

I suggest that you start with your bedtime routine because getting enough sleep every day will make it much easier to remember and learn all of the other skills we've told you about.

Keep a record with your mom or dad so that you can chart your progress. The record can be a simple calendar where you make a check mark on each day that you are successful in practicing your new skill.

The better you get at each skill, the better you will feel. Your days will go more smoothly and you won't feel rushed or upset that you've forgotten something important.

Good luck! You can do it!

Note to Parents

LEARNING the skills that are called "executive functioning" (EF) skills are critical to success later in life. This book focuses on the executive functioning skills related to developing good daily time management routines, keeping belongings in order, and planning and carrying out projects.

Tips for Teaching EF Skills

Below are some more tips for helping your child learn EF skills.

Set reachable goals.

The mistake most parents are prone to make when trying to teach EF skills to their child is to have unrealistic expectations about how quickly their child can learn these skills and how much support they will need over the years to consistently develop such skills. Set small, reachable goals and reward your child's improvement.

Seek support for yourself.

If you are a parent that finds it difficult to be organized and follow daily routines yourself, then teaching these skills to your child becomes a double challenge. If you find it difficult to consistently implement and support daily routines with your child, the best approach may be to work with a coach yourself who can support you in supporting your child.

Think like a preschool teacher.

Isn't it amazing that 20 or more preschool children can come into their classroom and behave in an orderly fashion throughout the time they are at school? You'll never see jackets flung on the floor or plates and cups left on random surfaces. In the preschool, toys are not left in a jumble.

Order reigns. Think about how preschool teachers and aides accomplish this and you'll be well on your way to achieving a high level of order in your home.

- Have a place where jackets, backpacks, and lunch containers go—then make sure they go there!
- Have clearly labeled boxes, drawers, and baskets where each item clearly belongs. Don't allow your child to keep so many toys, items of clothing, and art projects that there is no clear, organized place for them to be stored.
- Give immediate reminders. Immediate reminders and corrections are needed, over and over, until these acts become automatic for your child.
- Reminders should be neutral or encouraging. Praise your child over and over for doing it right.

Bring your child into the process of planning and organizing.

This way, new routines and expectations are not just something imposed by you. Have your child help you to create reminder lists for morning routines, after-school routines, and bedtime routines—they can illustrate them, color them, anything to make them their own. Then, laminate them and hang each routine prompt in a conspicuous place.

Make chores a family time.

It's a lot more fun to do chores when everyone is pitching in. For example, you could have one child set the table while an older child empties the dishwasher. Or one child could feed the family pets while another child does "trash patrol"—emptying all of the waste baskets into a large bag to take outside to the trash cans.

Reward Your Child

Reward your child for success in following daily routines. Remember:

- Small, immediate rewards are more effective than bigger rewards that take longer to reach. Make it easy to earn rewards. The more your child succeeds, the harder she will try.
- A combination of small, immediate rewards and points toward a bigger reward can be even more effective.

- Be very clear about how your child earns rewards and points—write it down so that there is no misunderstanding. The last thing you want to do is to create an upset because there was a misunderstanding about how she can earn a reward.
- Reward improvement, not perfection!
- Set reachable goals with your child. If you set a goal that is too hard to reach you will only discourage yourself and your child. Even a *huge* reward won't help your child reach a goal that is too big a change. Take change step by step and celebrate every small sign of improvement.
- Don't try to change too many things at once. Most of us can only work on 2-3 things at a time.
- Kids with AD/HD do better if they have visual reminders. Try taking some of the lists in this book and making a copy to post in their room or on the refrigerator to help them remember. This book contains forms and checklists for building a new habit; creating a morning, after-school, and bedtime routine; and planning a project. These forms are available as free downloadable PDFs on the book's page on Magination Press's website: www.apa.org/pubs/magination.
- Try to make the rewards happen when and where the behavior happens.

- Get the support that you need as a parent to be calm, consistent, and encouraging as you work with your child to develop new habits.
- Remember, changing is hard work. Don't emphasize set-backs. Instead, focus on improvements, however small. For example, if your child has a huge upset, but comes back to apologize, focus on the apology. Congratulate your child for calming down and coming back to apologize. Encourage them and tell them that you can see they are doing better. Don't over-focus on the upset. Help your child problem-solve to see if you can find a way to avoid an upset next time.

The most rewarding thing that you can offer your child is positive one-on-one time. Don't get caught up in giving your child too many sweets or costly items. There are many very rewarding things you can do that are healthy for your child and won't break the family budget. For example:

- Play a card game or board game with your child.
- Give permission to have a play date.
- Do a cooking project together.
- Play a computer game with your child.
- Watch a DVD together.
- Make popcorn necklaces with your child—then eat them!
- Allow your child to watch a half-hour of TV after homework is done.

- Get a "free pass" from doing a chore.
- Order a pizza on Friday night if your child has had a better week.
- Let your child stay up an hour later on a week-end night.
- Let your child have a sleep-over as a reward for a good week.
- Go bike-riding with your child.
- Play catch with your child.
- Read your child an extra story at bedtime.
- Give your child a special back-rub at bedtime.

Encourage Your Child

Be generous with your encouragement. Your child will thrive on positive feedback, such as:

- Hugs
- Pats
- Smiles
- "Way to go!"
- "Great job!"
- "I know how hard you are trying."
- "I'm proud of you."

Plan Special Time With Your Child

"Special time" is different from reward time. Research shows that as little as five minutes each day of special time can make a huge positive difference in your relationship with your child.

Special time is a time for you to just sit with your child as he or she sits and plays. Creative toys that don't have rules or points make the best special time activities—dolls, puppets, and Legos or other construction toys work well.

During special time your role is to:

- Reflect: "You're building a tower!"
- Praise the child's activity: "What a great tower you're building!"
- Describe: "Oh, now you're building a bridge to the tower."
- Enjoy: smile and show your child how much you enjoy his or her company during this special time.

During special time, don't criticize, instruct, question, or give advice. This is a time for your child to bask in your undivided attention while doing an activity in which there is no right or wrong.

Think of this special time as a "medicine" that your child needs every day. On days when there has been more conflict, special time is even more important.

Resources

If your child struggles with organizing, planning, remembering, and consistency, look for as much support as you can find. Often, these struggles are related to learning or attentional problems. Be sure that your child has received a comprehensive assessment so that all issues are being addressed.

Below, you'll find a list of organizations and online resources that may be helpful to you as you look for supports for yourself and your child.

WEBSITES FOR FINDING A COACH

Many coaches can work with parents and their children together to help them build and maintain their planning and organizing skills. To find coaches that have been trained and certified, try these websites. Even if your child has not been diagnosed with AD/HD, coaches that specialize in AD/HD coaching are especially trained in helping people to improve their executive functioning skills and therefore can be most helpful to your child.

AD/HD Coaches Organization
www.ADHDcoaches.org

American Coaching Association
www.americoach.org

International Coaches Federation
www.coachfederation.org

WEBSITES FOR FINDING A CHILD OR FAMILY THERAPIST

If you and your child find yourselves in frequent and intense conflicts over your efforts to introduce better daily routines and planning techniques, it may be helpful to bring in a child and family specialist to help you learn ways to interact with your child that are calmer and more productive.

American Psychological Association
www.apa.org

National Register of Health Care Providers in Psychology
www.findapsychologist.org

OTHER HELPFUL WEBSITES

The following websites are filled with a trove of helpful articles for parents of disorganized kids:

ADDitude Magazine
www.additudemag.com
ADDitude Magazine is a publication that supports families affected by AD/HD. Each publication contains helpful organizing tips for parents and kids.

Center for Collaborative Problem Solving
www.ccps.info
Ross Green's approach is particularly effective and helpful when there is an ongoing power struggle between parent and child that is getting in the way of productive problem solving. His approach helps parents and kids get on the same side of the table, problem solving together.

Learning Disabilities Association of America
www.ldaamerica.org
The Learning Disabilities Association of America is an organization to support children with learning differences as well as their families and educators. Parents can find advice and resources that can help them improve their child's executive functioning skills.

Understood
www.Understood.org
This site offers a wealth of information for parents. It was formed by a group of professionals as a non-profit organization whose goal is to provide parents with in-depth and highly useful information to help their child with learning or attentional problems.

HELPFUL WEB ARTICLES TO HELP KIDS GET ORGANIZED

Garvey, A. "Organizing with Kids" Pinterest board. Retrieved from: https://www.pinterest.com/abygarvey/organizing-with-kids/

Marrero, L. (2015, July 13). 9 smart ways to make kids more organized. *Good Housekeeping.* Retrieved from http://www.goodhousekeeping. com/home/organizing/tips/g340/organizing-tips-for-kids/

Morin, A. (n. d.). 7 tips for organizing your child's backpack. *Understood.* Retrieved from https://www.understood.org/en/school-learning/ learning-at-home/teaching-organizational-skills/7-tips-for-organizing-your-childs-backpack

Wright, L. W. (n. d.). 10 tips to help your child get organized. Understood. Retrieved from https://www.understood.org/en/learning-attention-issues/understanding-childs-challenges/simple-changes-at-home/10-tips-to-help-get-your-child-organized

BOOKS FOR PARENTS

Goldberg, D. & Zwiebel, J. (2005). *The organized student: Teaching children the skills for success in school and beyond.* New York, NY: Touchstone.

Gordon, R. M. (2007). *Thinking organized for parents and children: Helping kids get organized for home, school and play.* Chevy Chase, MD. Thinking Organized.

Kutscher, M. & Moran, M. (2009). *Organizing the disorganized child.* New York: Harper Collins.

Spizman, R. F. & Garber, M. D. (2000). *Helping kids get organized: Activities that teach time management, clutter clearing, project planning, and more!* Columbus, OH: Good Apple.

BOOKS FOR KIDS

Espeland, P. & Verdick, E. (2007). *See you later, procrastinator! (Get it done).* Golden Valley, MN: Free Spirit.

Fox, J. S. (2007). *Get organized without losing it.* Golden Valley, MN: Free Spirit.

Muchnick, C. C. (2011). *The everything guide to study skills: Strategies, tips, and tools you need to succeed in school!* Avon, MA: Adams Media.

Verdick, E. (2010). *Don't behave like you live in a cave.* Golden Valley, MN: Free Spirit.

About the Author

Kathleen G. Nadeau, PhD, is a clinical psychologist who has specialized in working with kids and adults with AD/HD for many years. She is the founder and director of the Chesapeake ADHD Center in Silver Spring, MD, and the author of many books on AD/HD for kids, teens, adults, and professionals. She has been a pioneer in bringing recognition to girls and women with AD/HD, and is known for her positive focus and practical problem-solving treatment approach. Dr. Nadeau is a frequent lecturer on topics related to AD/HD, both in the United States and abroad.

About the Illustrator

Charles Beyl creates humorous illustrations for books, magazines, and newspapers in his suburban Texas ranch house. When he's not drawing, you'll find him wrangling his pug, riding his bike, or dodging mosquitos.

About Magination Press

Magination Press is an imprint of the American Psychological Association, the largest scieantific and professional organization representing psychologists in the United States and the largest association of psychologists worldwide.